FOR THE DREAMERS

A POETIC COLLECTION

OF LOVE

GEORGE SPENDLEY

TRAFFORD PUBLISHING
VICTORIA, BC, CANADA

Designed by George Spendley and Scott Peterson.
Photographs by George Spendley with the exception of page 84 by Patty Peavey and page 96 by Mary Ledford.

Canadian Cataloguing in Publication Data

Spendley, George, 1949-
For the dreamers

Poems.
Includes index.
ISBN 1-55212-311-1

I. Title.
PS3569.P37F67 2000 811'.54 C99-911325-9

TRAFFORD

This book was published *on-demand* in cooperation with Trafford Publishing.
On-demand publishing is a unique process and service of making a book available for retail sale to the public taking advantage of on-demand manufacturing and Internet marketing. **On-demand publishing** includes promotions, retail sales, manufacturing, order fulfilment, accounting and collecting royalties on behalf of the author.

Suite 6E - 2333 Government St., Victoria, B.C. V8T 4P4, CANADA
Phone 250-383-6864 Toll-free 1-888-232-4444 (Canada & US)
Fax 250-383-6804 E-mail sales@trafford.com
Web site www.trafford.com TRAFFORD PUBLISHING IS A DIVISION OF TRAFFORD HOLDINGS LTD.
Trafford Catalogue #99-0061 www.trafford.com/robots/99-0061.html

10 9 8 7 6 5 4 3

To my family.

ACKNOWLEDGEMENTS

I would like to give thanks to the following people: Paula Belliveau, Lou Blanton, Kathryn Carr, Sam Colt, Jan Ebelke, Nancy Godbout-Jurka, Kathy Hall, Debbi-ruth Hobbs, and Debby Kohler for their encouragement and belief in me; to Mary Ledford and Patty Peavey for allowing the use of their photographs of John Denver; and to John Denver, who showed me the gift of the written word as poetry. I give special thanks to Carolyn Reineke Matthews for showing me the vision of my poems in print; and to Scott Peterson for his assistance in the design and production of this book.

Most importantly, I thank my family for their unconditional love and support.

CONTENTS

INTRODUCTION

I am a dreamer. When I was first told this, it was meant to make me feel as though I wasn't applying myself seriously to anything. It was said to make me feel that I was wasting my time instead of putting it to a good, productive use. One of my first inspirations to put anything into writing came from this declaration to me. I was thirteen years old. I bought a greeting card with the painting of a child sitting on a branch high in a tree, daydreaming. The inside of the card was blank. Using an old Smith Corona typewriter, I typed my own thoughts inside the card. "People tell me I'm a dreamer. Can you tell me why I should settle for anything less than my dreams?"

Over the years I never gave it much thought whether I was still a dreamer or if I had settled into an adulthood of practicality and reason. A close friend pointed out to me recently that the majority of the poems on my website relate to dreams. It was at that moment that I realized I will always be a dreamer, and I still ask...why should anyone settle for less than their dreams?

These thoughts and feelings that I express through my written words of poetry...are truly for the dreamers.

- George Spendley

OakCreekPoetry@aol.com
http://members.xoom.com/oakcreekpoet

****

"These are the poems of George Spendley.... spoken from his heart and his life's experiences. As a dreamer, his voice has a vision.... with words to be written.... and a heart to share. He weaves his words together.... for the lover.... for the seeker.... for the wild outdoors..for the child.... and for the 'John Denver' in all of us.... in a most passionate and simplistic way. His poetry takes you on a journey from Colorado's mountains to Alaska's rivers..to the sea with God's creatures. George's words bring you home to his life as a father..and of his admiration for John Denver. He blends his heart with passion and pain as love and life crosses between daydreams and reality. Let his words and his heart take you on your own journey...with For The Dreamers."

- Nancy Godbout-Jurka

****

"A dreamer loves to dream. A dreamer loves to soar. Nothing is more satisfying than to be taken away on a momentary, magical mind trip. George Spendley is able to capture these journey's through the mind. His words reach deep inside and carry one to where he is. As a dreamer myself, I find 'peace' when reading his poetry : a bit of love on this planet Earth."

- Debbi-ruth Hobbs

****

****

"George has the ability to write romantic poetry using descriptive phrases which 'take you places', awakening your senses and emotions. You will laugh as you read 'Internet Love' and shed sentimental tears reading his poems about home and family. You'll experience his joy and love of nature; feel the wind, smell the summer rain, and see the golden aspen leaves quaking in the trees. To read his poetry is to know George Spendley. He writes from his heart and his heart is in every poem. A very dear, close friend, George has been an inspiration in my life. Through his words and his heart, he taught me how to 'listen' so that I, too, could write......and become one of the dreamers."

- Carolyn Reineke Matthews

****

For The Lovers....

COOL WHISPER

There's a coolness that instills a peace deep within
as the breeze slowly enters my room.
My thoughts wander far to the garden you grace;
a sweetness is carried with each fragrant bloom.

This cool gentleness that I feel on my neck,
does it come from the touch of the air?
Or is it your whisper reminding me of
the love and the passion we share?

Near the window I sit as I turn to look out
to watch the leaves quake in the trees.
But the air is now still, the leaves do not move,
as I listen to hear your voice speak to me.

The distance between us seems endless at times
when I long for your smile and your touch.
Once more this gentleness caresses my neck,
this cool whisper reminds me....I love you so much.

AFTERGLOW

And so we breathe easy as you lay in my arms,
our hearts still pounding with love.
You've left me light-headed with each of your charms,
your skin so soft, like the wings of a dove.

The passion we share has surpassed what is real,
we lay with no need to speak.
For there are no words to describe how we feel,
we drift into pleasure that's left us both weak.

To hold you, to touch you, to stroke your soft hair
is all that I live for right now.
I place gentle kisses on a face that's so fair,
and pray that this night lasts forever somehow.

AS AUTUMN NEARS

The time is quick approaching
when the leaves all turn to gold,
as autumn sneaks upon us,
as the skies grow gray and cold.

The wind would be so lonely
if I didn't have you near;
these nights would last forever
but you whisper in my ear.

"Stay close and hold me tightly,
let me be your comfort now.
The sun will rise tomorrow
and we'll get through this somehow."

The storm clouds overcome us,
there is fear that we will cry.
But know that love's forever
with no need to question why.

FOR THE DREAMERS

He lives on a mountain,

though not at the top,

for the top is a place for the dreamers.

He sits on a throne,

though he is not King,

for the King is the one who oversees dreamers.

He cries in his heart,

though his heart is kind,

for the kindness is what enlightens the dreamers.

He speaks of a love,

though the love is not perfect,

for a perfect love is the dream of the dreamers.

TWELVE DAYS OF LOVE

One night, two hearts,

three days, four apart,

five dances, six songs,

seven rights, eight wrongs,

nine wishes, ten proposes,

eleven yes's, twelve roses.

DAWN TO DAY

Just before dawn,

moonlight gracing our room,

you awaken me with a kiss.

Outside, stars fall

through darkened, cloudless skies;

you lead me to promising bliss.

With silent stares

past eyes into the soul,

love speaks what our hearts deeply know.

The moonlight fades,

shadows caress your skin,

as sunrise shows our love's sweet glow.

UNIVERSAL MENDER

Duct tape on my broken chair,
duct tape on my lamp,
duct tape on my sleeping bag,
duct tape when I camp.

Duct tape on my garden hose,
duct tape on my phone,
duct tape in my horse's stall,
duct tape in my home.

Duct tape on my stereo,
duct tape on my bed,
duct tape wrapped around my leg,
duct tape on my head.

Duct tape on my cowboy boots,
duct tape on my car,
all the duct tape in the world
won't mend my broken heart.

HIS AND HERS

Love of kindness,

love of joy,

love of celebration.

Heart of darkness,

heart of fear,

heart of no emotion.

Love of longing,

love of hope,

love with dedication.

Heart of aching,

heart of pain,

heart with no devotion.

INTERNET LOVE

Who would have thought we'd fall in love
the day that we first met,
that moment that I saw your name
here on the internet.

I'd rush to sign on everyday
to read your mail to me.
But lightning hit and knocked me out
and dropped me to my knees.

It took my modem and my screen,
there was static in the air.
I lost a thumb, my nose went numb,
it even fried my hair.

I tried to save my CD's
and I grabbed each floppy disk.
I tried to save my poems for you,
I really took a risk.

Another bolt of lightning
made my mouse fly way up high
and on it's way back to the desk,
it poked me in the eye.

Since then my system's been repaired
with many brand new parts.
I'm grateful I still have my toes
but damn, I lost my heart!

PHOTOGRAPH

I have a special photograph
I look at now and then;
reminds me of the time back then
when we were such good friends.

We used to lay awake at night
and talk about our dreams.
We'd build a cabin in the woods
and light it with moonbeams.

We'd go for rides on winter nights,
the air was crisp and cold.
The sky was filled...a million stars,
just one I'd like to hold.

We drank hot wine by candlelight
and listened to our songs,
but sometimes love does funny things,
and who knows what went wrong?

But I have this special photograph
I look at now and then;
reminds me of the time back then,
I thought we were good friends.

QUESTIONS

Who was the one who broke your heart?
Who was the one before me?
Who was the one who tore you apart
and left all the pieces to see?

Why do you cry when I tell you I care?
Why do you doubt all my words?
Why do you think that love isn't fair
when I know that each word has been heard?

When will you let the past slip away?
When will you let yourself give?
When will you open yourself to the day
and allow yourself courage to live?

ROYAL DAYS AND KNIGHTS

In this land of our late King
now rules a gracious Queen.
At her request, a gathering,
great horsemen can be seen.

Rounds of jousts with common men
who seek to become knights,
risk life and love as they begin
each fierce and deadly fight.

And with a feast we celebrate
this season now upon us.
Wine is sipped as we partake
in pleasures far beyond us.

Gentlemen and ladies fair
walk quiet in the night.
Seeking passion, if they dare,
in warm embrace beneath star's light.

FOR YOU

With thoughts of you

keeping me awake

I wonder how you must be.

I have no right

to think of you

for we have yet to meet.

But if I were of liberated spirit

and thought you of the same,

I'd ask you now to join me

in a lifetime filled with wine.

TRUSTING HEARTS

As we met I wondered
if a friendship would be formed,
for trusting hearts are easy,
even if they've been forewarned.

Perhaps we'd even fall in love
and plan our future days,
or find that there was nothing here
and go our separate ways.

We only had a few short months,
still, time enough for you
to win my trust and honesty,
I thought I had yours, too.

But time has ways of showing light
and truth on hearts not warm,
for trusting hearts are broken
even when they've been forewarned.

SEASONS OF LOVE

Summer came, summer went,
golden days with you I spent.
On the shore, in the sand,
quiet walks, hand in hand.

Autumn days, cool clear nights,
we would love, we would fight.
Winter snow, now so cold,
longing for my love to hold.

Spring arrives, you're not near,
shattered dreams with every tear.
Love was mine, now is gone,
my heart sings a broken song.

TURN TO ME

When darkness overshadows
all your hopes and all your dreams,
when there's no one close to hold you
in the light of soft moonbeams,
when the music has stopped playing
but the song stays in your heart,
turn to me for love and comfort
and the promise we won't part.

SUMMER'S CHILD

Summer's child, with eyes of green,
most precious beauty that I've seen;
I beg, don't wake me from this dream...
my love belongs to you.

Summer's breeze graces the air,
gently brushes your soft hair,
bless me with your loving stare...
my heart belongs to you.

Summer's night in your embrace,
tender kisses I do place
softly on your lovely face...
my soul belongs to you.

THREE WORDS

Two lovers reach across endless spaces
hoping to touch in their heart's deepest places.
Echoes of love sound across the miles,
and to each face brings a gentle smile.

Two lovers long for their strongest desire
to hold one another near an evening fire.
Thoughts that are spoken, yet cannot be heard,
remain in their hearts with three simple words.

SWEET DREAMS

Sunny days, rainy nights,
cloudy skies, dimming lights.
Music plays, candles burn,
love is ours, my heart yearns.
Hold me tight, pull me near,
words of love speak in my ear.
Kisses soft, sweet caress,
my heart pounds, you undress.
By my side, sleep with me,
in my arms, love's sweet dreams.

LESSONS

Teach me a lesson in honesty

Teach me a lesson in pain

Teach me a lesson in love that is lost

And I swear it won't happen again.

IMMUNE

To take a chance

and open my heart

may leave a space

only to be filled by a cold draft.

So here I'll stay

where the temperature is always the same,

immune from catching

a bad cold.

DECISIONS OF EXPECTATIONS

Decisions made of expectations,

those of others.....not their own,

divides one love into two separate hearts

sent to different worlds that are now numb.

Both lonely.....both knowing.....

decisions made of expectations

pleases all.....

except themselves.

For The Children...

COUNT YOUR BLESSINGS

Count your blessings one by one,
never let them go.
Take for granted not one day
but treasure them as gold.

Live each day as though the last;
watch the morning sun.
Touch a flower, feel the petals,
soft and fragile are each one.

Dream about tomorrow's promise,
cherish days gone by.
Take whatever fate may bring you;
then release it, let it fly.

Count your blessings one by one,
never let them go.
In your heart you know the answers,
open up and let love flow.

NEWBORN

Grasp of tiny newborn hand

gives unto my heart

strength and courage now to cry.

ANNIE NOELLE

On this day a baby girl

was brought into this joyous world.

With hair so fair and eyes so blue,

a smile so bright, a heart so true.

A blessed gift from One above,

for in this child bestows His love.

SNOWFLAKES

A child is born,
a baby cries.
With pride and joy
a mother sighs.

A snowflake falls,
an angel smiles.
A song is heard
across the miles.

A child is born,
a life brand new.
A family shares
a dream come true.

A snowflake falls,
...an angel's tear,
of love and hope
for many years.

ROOM OF DREAMS

In this room that holds our dreams,
the hopes of future, all that means
the world to us and then much more,
a baby's cry beyond the door.
A precious gift receives our love
sent down to us from God above.
A little girl whose soul is pure,
whose love and laughter will ensure
a home that's filled with warmth and peace;
she lays upon her bed of fleece.
For in this room that holds our dreams
a baby's smile can now be seen.

CHRISTMAS JOY

Christmas eve
late night snow
fireplace
burning slow

Blue spruce tree
twinkling lights
baby's eyes
wide and bright

Morning frost
windows glazed
scent of pine
Christmas Day.

IN YOUR MOTHER'S EYES

I see you in your mother's eyes
and in the moon's pure light.
I see you in a summer's day,
I see you in the night.

I see you through the pane of glass,
I see your face so small.
I see you in your mother's arms,
the wonder of it all.

I see you standing by my side,
I see your smile so bright.
I see your little hand in mine,
I feel you squeeze so tight.

I see you with the man you love,
I see you sip the wine.
I see you take his name for life,
this little girl of mine.

I see you in your mother's eyes,
I see you in the wild.
I see you in the moonlit sky,
this precious dear grandchild.

For The Seekers....

BEFORE THIS

In a life before this
our souls were in touch,
our bodies together,
our love meant so much.

In a life before this
our passions were shared,
our spirits ran deep,
for our earth we both cared.

In a life before this
we walked arm in arm
through forests or deserts,
in lands filled with harm.

In a life before this
our souls made a vow
to find one another
as each lifetime allows.

DAYDREAMS

My eyes absorb the desert sky
as twilight turns to black.
Within my mind I'm on the moon,
but then you call me back.

The evening warmth caresses me,
again I long to roam.
I hear your voice speak words of love
reminding me of home.

To journey through the stars above
becomes a dream of peace.
You set me free to find my soul,
my spirit within reach.

IN THE DARKNESS

Here in the darkness
that comes from within,
surrounding my spirit,
I let no light in.

To be so alone,
so deep within fear,
I listen for voices
but none do I hear.

Confusion prevails,
these thoughts in the night,
I search for the answers,
I wait for the light.

For I am the darkness
as I am the pain,
and I am the storm cloud,
for I am the rain.

CAROLYN

Her spirit was hidden
from even herself
'til she searched her heart one day.
And what she discovered
she already knew,
it had been there to guide her way.

Through times of joy
and times of pain,
and times of darkest nights.
When no one there
knew what she felt,
his music was the comforting light.

Her spirit has risen
to the highest of heights,
for spirits do always shine through.
Together they soar
over mountains and streams,
as we all know that dreams do come true.

FLIGHT

On winds so soft

between Heaven and Earth,

I balance on a breeze.

HANG-GLIDER

Like an eagle you soar over tree-covered mountains
Your wings are backed by the sun's tender rays
And the colors of rainbows shine down upon us
To touch those below who watch you in play.

A raindrop falls from a gray cloud above you
Missing your wings on it's way to the ground
A collection of clouds form a laser-like mist
An unorganized rainbow as you float around.

As quick as the rain starts, then stops again
A new cloud forms, taking shape at your side
You drift through the clouds keeping count of each one
'Til your flight is completed with the end of your glide.

HOME

Where is your home,
is it where you were born?
Or where time was spent most
until you were torn
away from the years and
the memories you had -
or is it a place
where it makes you feel glad?
A place where you're safe
and secure, and you're known;
a space in your heart
when it tells you you're 'home'.

LOST SOUL

Lost in my heart, lost in my soul,
lost in the part that once made me whole.
Lost in my pride, lost among friends,
there in my stride was the fear of no end.

Hearts that are broken, theirs and my own,
words that were spoken now fall like a stone.
"The man has such charm, he speaks oh, so sweet."
"He means us no harm. I wish we could meet."

Too many voices, and too many ways
to make the wrong choices to cause painful days.
This road that I take down a long lonesome path,
I know I must make through my heart's aftermath.

QUIET FOOTSTEPS

He walked with quiet footsteps
into areas unknown,
seeking love and comfort,
friendships solid as a stone.

Or so they seemed to all he met
as days passed quickly by,
with secrets shared and trusting hearts
and countless little lies.

He walks with quiet footsteps now
through the aftermath of pain.
Not worthy of such tender friends,
retreating once again.

ROADS

Roads that I have traveled,

roads still yet to come,

roads that lead to nowhere,

roads that are not done.

Roads of lonely highway,

roads of empty dreams,

roads that follow heartache,

roads that spoke to me.

Roads of ancient history,

roads for future days,

roads lit up with starlight,

roads to guide my way.

YEARS

For years and years I lived in the city
with concrete yards and fences of steel.
Skies were brown with the breath of the cars
with maniacs seated behind every wheel.

For thirty-odd years I lived in the city
where buildings were being constructed each day;
ones going straight up and some to the side,
a 'paradise' full of cement and clay.

For too many years I lived in the city
where the national pastime is standing in line.
Where they changed the name from Friday to Payday
and on Payday they play the national pastime.

For years and years I wanted to go
where skies are blue and trees grow free.
And now is the time for dreams to come true,
it's time to go home and find peace for me.

SUNRISE, SUNSET

As you are the sunrise, I am the setting sun.
As you greet the dawn of day,
I say goodnight when day is done.

As you are the sunrise, and I the fall of night,
you bring the warmth of summer days;
I bring the moon to make it bright.

As you are the sunrise, I am the bright sunset.
You plan the day for lovers all,
I plan the night for lover's rest.

SEEKERS

There are those who seek enlightenment
and those who seek their soul,
those who seek untimely answers,
questions still unfold.

Those who walk on water,
those who cannot see,
those who pass through every day
who still can't let things be.

Those who share the laughter,
those who hide the pain,
those whose hearts are broken
who can never love again.

Those who seek the wisdom
other men have known,
those like me who wonder
if they ever will be shown.

A CONVERSATION

"You're going to miss it,

wait and see.

The city is the place to be."

"I'll get over it,

I'll survive,

I'll be in the mountains...

I'll be alive!"

MISUNDERSTANDINGS

He thinks he's flower child,

nature child,

John Denver,

child of wonder.

Euell Gibbons,

Rumplestiltskin,

Lewis and Clark expedition.

For The Wild Things....

ALAGNAK

I know of this place, for I've been here before,
although this is my first journey.
I know of this river, this wildness surrounds me,
where my spirit and heart for so long have been yearning.

I know of each ripple, each movement of water,
each rock that creates a small wave.
I know of the creatures who walk here among me
allowing me space in the calm of their day.

I know of this land and this blue sky above me,
the eagles that fly overhead.
I know of this feeling that stirs deep within me,
this peace causes tears of joy to be shed.

I know now the purpose, the reason behind it;
Alaska, this country, this river Alagnak.
I know that my being, my soul and my spirit,
by nature and earth, have been welcomed back.

OF MAN AND HORSE

Connecting souls as brown eyes meet,
the horse and man stand firm to greet
each other with man's gentle hands
on quivering skin that understands.

Their hearts are kind, respect runs deep,
a trust is formed, a bond to keep.
Across the open range they ride
together in the horse's stride,
to reach the sun that sets so low
and solitude they've come to know.

RAIN

From time to time

rain will come

to wash away memories of summer.

IN THE FOREST

The eyes of the forest
sees the beauty within,
while the ears of the forest
hears it's music begin.

The heart of the forest
seeks peace for all beings,
while the soul of the forest
is wise and all-seeing.

My eyes see the forest
being cut down in size,
while my ears in the forest
hear the trees and their cries.

My heart feels the forest,
the pain runs so deep,
while my soul is the forest,
it's for us that I weep.

GARDENS

In gardens of dreams

you turn to smile

as peace enters my heart.

KAITLYN'S PONIES

Thundering hooves across the land,
the ponies make their strongest stand
against the sky they roam so free,
through mountain fields they race for me.

The chestnut mare with flaxen mane
runs with the wind into the rain.
She canters with such style and grace
while others try to keep her pace.

White stallion grazes in meadow nearby,
then raises his head to watch the hawk fly
above his herd, above the great mare,
their souls have met within their stare.

Horses and hawks, their hooves and wings,
bring timeless wonders to all living things.
To race with the wind, to fly high in peace,
are dreams of mine one day I will reach.

THUNDER

Gray skies roll

like ocean waves

as thunder speaks its voice to us.

THE MOUNTAIN SEA

The wind comes and goes
like the ocean tide,
crashing through aspen trees
on my mountainside.

Breaking on the branches,
waves upon the shore,
bringing leaves of aspens
to the forest floor.

Sweeping up their spirits,
not sure where to go,
gathered by each wave of wind
continuing to blow.

An annual migration,
clannads of ocean waves
rushing through my mountains
on their way to autumn days.

STARS

As stars appear
as a blanket overhead,
so too, my love covers you.

MOUNTAIN MUSIC

Can you hear the music in the mountains just begin?
Does the rhythm of the forest and the beauty that's within,
as the song of Mother Wind passes by you on a breeze,
make you happy and contented as you dance to it with ease?

Can you touch the clouds above you as they gently pass you by;
do you look at them with wonder without ever knowing why?
Do the heavens and the stars above shine down on us with grace?
If they do then I believe that they shine down upon your face.

SEASONS REBORN

In my ears
I hear the wind
sing her song of winter days.

In my eyes
I see the branches
welcome snowflakes to stay.

In my hands
I feel the warmth
that hides behind the coldness of the snow.

And in my heart
I know the season
reflects my desire to be reborn in the spring.

MOTHER WIND

The wind rushes across the forest
as it rushes through my mind.
I hear her calling me,
speaking to my spirit.

The answer is in my soul
with thoughts she cannot hear,
but the connection is strong
...there is no need to speak.

COLORADO WONDER

Whenever I'm lonely and feeling despair

I think why I came here and why I still care.

I step outside and take it all in,

the mountains, the blue sky, and time and again

the feeling of loneliness passes me by.

I think why I came here, and then start to cry.

THE SONG OF THE WHALE

The song of the whale
is a lonely song.
The cries of the pod
as they venture along
sing messages told of days long ago
when freedom was theirs
and the sea was so bold.

The song of the whale
is a desperate song.
Long ships armed with men,
with a greed that is strong,
seek to destroy gentle creatures so mild.
There's blindness in men
robbing earth of it's wild.

The song of the whale
is the song of my heart.
They sing to us all
if we take time to start
to teach all mankind that the song that we hear
is the song of our soul,
should we choose to hold dear.

LEAVES

Colorful leaf-spirits from trees

grace the breezes of

cool mountain autumn days.

WINTER

Winter brings a solitude,
a time for contemplation.
Ice crystals glisten
where once was a quaking leaf.
Footprints scatter across powdered snow
from tiny creatures at play.
Stillness can be heard
by those who take time to listen....
and learn.

Winter brings warmth of love
of families gathered together.
Fireside comfort, flames of many colors
glowing in the reflection of eyes
that hold the secrets to my heart.
A time of peace, of slowing down
the quickening pace of year after year,
for those who take time to listen....
and learn.

John Denver, Red Rocks, Colorado 1989
Photo by Patty Peavey

In Memory

of

John Denver....

THE GIFT OF THE SONG

In dark days of sadness and bright days of joy,
a gift of the music from a country boy
fills hearts all around with such passion and love,
it falls down upon us from Heaven above.

He taught us to dream, he taught us to hope,
he taught us to love and he taught us to cope.
Together we laughed, together we cried,
through words and through music we all shared the pride.

The days now grow shorter, the nights are so long,
but together we stay in the gift of the song.
The country boy's magic and love fills us all,
together, embraced, we prepare for the fall.

THE GATHERING

We are gathered here together
in this comfort, holding hands,
some seek love, some seek wisdom,
some a way to understand.

Remembering a day so dark,
and yet a life so bright,
how it touches each and every one,
his music and his light.

We are gathered here together
under Colorado skies,
knowing all too well the heartache
with the tears that fill our eyes.

LOVE-LIGHT

The days were warmed with sunshine
as his music filled the air.
We lived our lives from day to day,
we didn't have a care.

We thought our world would stay the same,
we knew there'd be next year.
We never gave it any thought,
that day would be so near.

The news spread fast as teardrops fell
and hearts broke one by one.
We sat in silent disbelief,
it seemed his life was done.

But as we shared our pain and grief
we each began to know
his life goes on in all our hearts,
it thrives in love-light's glow.

He lives in every one of us.
He lives in you and me.
He lives in Colorado skies.
He lives within a breeze.

He lives in children seen at play.
He lives in streams so clear.
He lives in hearts around the world,
in music we still hear.

So when you feel the pain approach,
remember days so sweet,
and carry on his legacy
'til once again we meet.

TIME

Time has no meaning,
it passes me by.
What once was December
could now be July.

From minutes to hours
and days into weeks,
I look back at yesterday,
tears on my cheeks.

What will be tomorrow
is all today's dreams,
as forgotten memories
slip away with a breeze.

Time has stood still
since that day long ago.
If time is for healing,
why must it be slow?

Time has no meaning,
it flies past my way.
What once was October
could now be today.

IF I COULD

If I could take away this pain you feel
then know I surely would.
I'd like to make you smile again
to see the love I should.

If I could mend all broken hearts
and make them laugh once more,
then know I'd start with my own heart,
and then I would mend yours.

If I could share all happiness
that hides within us all,
I'd open up my arms for you
and catch you when you fall.

If I could reach the stars and moon,
and give them all to you,
I'd gather each and every one
and make your dreams come true.

If I could turn the hands of time
and fill your vacant soul,
I'd give you back each day since then
when all our hearts were whole.

GIFTED HANDS

Gifted hands caressed strings

of musical notes

as hearts filled with his words.

PARTING WORDS

It's about love,
it's about life,
it's about sharing,
and it's about strife.

It's about people,
it's about dreams,
it's about forests,
and it's about streams.

It's about stars,
it's about sea,
it's about you,
and it's about me.

It's about war,
it's about peace,
it's about gladness,
and it's about grief.

It's about children,
it's about earth,
it's about flowers,
and it's about birth.

It's about caring,
it's about how,
and it's about giving,
...do you have it now?

COULD YOU HEAR IT?

When he thought no one was listening
he said that we should care.
When he thought no one was listening
he had wise words to share.

When he thought no one was listening
he spoke of Mother Earth.
When he thought no one was listening
came words of her true worth.

When he thought no one was listening
he sang of love and loss.
When he thought no one was listening
his message came across.

When he thought no one was listening
is when he gave us light.
When he thought no one was listening
we dreamed to soar his heights.

When he thought no one was listening
is when the children heard.
When he thought no one was listening
came truth of all his words.

When he thought no one was listening
his heart spoke for us all.
When he thought no one was listening
he tore down hatred's wall.

When they thought no one was listening
we heard a poet's voice.
When they thought no one was listening
his music was our choice.

When they thought no one was listening
his strength was in his words.
Though they still think no one's listening
his heart's heard 'round the world.

John Denver, Camden, New Jersey, 1995
Photo by Mary Ledford

www.ingramcontent.com/pod-product-compliance
Ingram Content Group UK Ltd.
Pitfield, Milton Keynes, MK11 3LW, UK
UKHW041845190726
13854UKWH00002B/725

9 781552 123119